D1258025

WITHDRAWN

3 1526 04320369 1

WRITER: **KIERON GILLEN**

#15-17 ARTIST: **DANIEL ACUÑA** WITH **MIKE DEL MUNDO** (#17)
ART ASSIST: **DIEGO OLMOS** (#17)

#18 ARTIST: **RON GARNEY**
COLORS: **JASON KEITH** & **MORRY HOLLOWELL**

#19 ARTIST: **DALE EAGLESHAM**
COLORS: **MATT MILLA**

#20 PENCILER: **CARLOS PACHECO**
INKS: **ROGER BONET** • COLORS: **GURU-eFX**

LETTERS: **VC'S JOE CARAMAGNA** • COVER ART: **DANIEL ACUÑA** (#15-16), **MIKE DEL MUNDO** (#17), **RON GARNEY** & **MATT MILLA** (#18-19); AND **CARLOS PACHECO, ROGER BONET** & **GURU-eFX** (#20)
ASSISTANT EDITOR: **JORDAN D. WHITE**
ASSOCIATE EDITOR: **DANIEL KETCHUM** • EDITOR: **NICK LOWE**

COLLECTION EDITOR: **JENNIFER GRÜNWALD** • ASSISTANT EDITORS: **ALEX STARBUCK** & **NELSON RIBEIRO**
EDITOR, SPECIAL PROJECTS: **MARK D. BEAZLEY** • SENIOR EDITOR, SPECIAL PROJECTS: **JEFF YOUNGQUIST**
SENIOR VICE PRESIDENT OF SALES: **DAVID GABRIEL**
SVP OF BRAND PLANNING & COMMUNICATIONS: **MICHAEL PASCIULLO**
BOOK DESIGNER: **RODOLFO MURAGUCHI**

EDITOR IN CHIEF: **AXEL ALONSO** • CHIEF CREATIVE OFFICER: **JOE QUESADA**
PUBLISHER: **DAN BUCKLEY** • EXECUTIVE PRODUCER: **ALAN FINE**

UNCANNY X-MEN BY KIERON GILLEN VOL. 4. Contains material originally published in magazine form as UNCANNY X-MEN #15-20. First printing 2012. Hardcover ISBN# 978-0-7851-6529-3. Softcover ISBN# 978-0-7851-6530-9. Published by MARVEL WORLDWIDE, INC., a subsidiary of MARVEL ENTERTAINMENT, LLC. OFFICE OF PUBLICATION: 135 West 50th Street, New York, NY 10020. Copyright © 2012 and 2013 Marvel Characters, Inc. All rights reserved. Hardcover: $24.99 per copy in the U.S. and $27.99 in Canada (GST #R127032852). Softcover: $19.99 per copy in the U.S. and $21.99 in Canada (GST #R127032852). Canadian Agreement #40668537. All characters featured in this issue and the distinctive names and likenesses thereof, and all related indicia are trademarks of Marvel Characters, Inc. No similarity between any of the names, characters, persons, and/or institutions in this magazine with those of any living or dead person or institution is intended, and any such similarity which may exist is purely coincidental. **Printed in the U.S.A.** ALAN FINE, EVP - Office of the President, Marvel Worldwide, Inc. and EVP & CMO Marvel Characters B.V.; DAN BUCKLEY, Publisher & President - Print, Animation & Digital Divisions; JOE QUESADA, Chief Creative Officer; TOM BREVOORT, SVP of Publishing; DAVID BOGART, SVP of Operations & Procurement, Publishing; RUWAN JAYATILLEKE, SVP & Associate Publisher, Publishing; C.B. CEBULSKI, SVP of Creator & Content Development; DAVID GABRIEL, SVP of Publishing Sales & Circulation; MICHAEL PASCIULLO, SVP of Brand Planning & Communications; JIM O'KEEFE, VP of Operations & Logistics; DAN CARR, Executive Director of Publishing Technology; SUSAN CRESPI, Editorial Operations Manager; ALEX MORALES, Publishing Operations Manager; STAN LEE, Chairman Emeritus. For information regarding advertising in Marvel Comics or on Marvel.com, please contact Niza Disla, Director of Marvel Partnerships, at ndisla@marvel.com. For Marvel subscription inquiries, please call 800-217-9158. **Manufactured between 10/1/2012 and 11/12/2012 (hardcover), and 10/1/2012 and 5/6/2013 (softcover), by R.R. DONNELLEY, INC., SALEM, VA, USA.**

10 9 8 7 6 5 4 3 2 1

Born with powers and abilities beyond those of normal humans, mutantkind has long been hated and feared by those they sought to protect. Now, from their island nation of Utopia, Cyclops leads the most powerful group of mutants ever assembled to protect what is left of his dwindling species. Hated and feared? When you are as powerful as the Uncanny X-Men, does it matter?

UNCANNY X-MEN

CYCLOPS
eye-blasting leader

EMMA FROST
telepath with diamond form

COLOSSUS
steel-skinned juggernaut

MAGIK
magic-using teleporter

NAMOR
king of Atlantis

MAGNETO
master of magnetism

DANGER
light-shaping AI

PSYLOCKE
telepathic ninja

STORM
weather witch

PREVIOUSLY

Mutantkind's ascension has begun. Following a battle with The Avengers, The Phoenix Force has been split into five separate parts, each one bonding with a member of the X-Men: Cyclops, Emma Frost, Colossus, Namor and Magik. Utilizing this power, they are rebuilding the world, solving its problems and building a better future.

Meanwhile, Mister Sinister has begun a new course of action against the X-Men. He has created an entire species of himself, all genetically perfect and identical Sinister clones. From his underground kingdom of Sinister London, he anticipates the X-Men's every move and eagerly awaits their attentions.

MAGIK?
COLOSSUS?

SOME THINGS EXIST ONLY TO BURN.

SINISTER IS AMONGST THEIR NUMBER.

VERY WELL. SCOTT?

YOU'VE BEEN QUIET.

WE'VE GOT THIS POWER. WE CAN MAKE A BETTER WORLD.

AND I THINK IT'D BE A BETTER WORLD WITHOUT SINISTER IN IT.

FIND HIM.

SINISTER LONDON, DEEP BENEATH THE EARTH'S SURFACE.

"SIR! SIR!"

THE PSYCHIC BATTALIONS REPORT THE PHOENIX-HOSTS ARE TRYING TO DIVINE OUR LOCATION.

IT BEGINS.

DISCONNECT THOSE MANNING THE SPIRES FROM THE HIVE MIND.

CONCEAL US FOR AS LONG AS THEY CAN MANAGE. HONOR THEM! THEY FIGHT A PSYCHIC THERMOPYLAE.

I'VE FOUND SOMETHING. THEY'RE RESISTING DISCOVERY.

PUSH HARDER.

WHERE IS THE ANNOYINGLY VERBOSE PREY?

HIS ABOMINATION OF A SPECIES IS FAR BELOW.

STILL, HE BAITS ME. THIS IS WHERE I GREW UP...WHERE HE FIRST WATCHED ME...

HE BRINGS ME BACK HERE...

...AS IF IT'S ALL STILL PART OF HIS PLAN.

HE MAKES A MISTAKE. HE THINKS US STILL HUMAN.

WHAT WE ARE NOW IS BEYOND HIS SMALL REASON.

THEY'VE BREACHED THE CAVERN.

EXCELLENT.

UNTETHER THE SPAWN! EMPTY THE MENAGERIE!

MARAUDER BATTALIONS ENGAGE! ENRAGE! ENFILADE!

AND US, YOUR MAJESTY?

WAIT, MADELYNE. YOUR TIME WILL COME.

FIRST THINGS FIRST.

THERE'S A SPECTACLE TO APPRECIATE.

AND DAMN ME, IF I SAY IT MYSELF...

ENOUGH. WE CAN'T JUST SIT HERE.

AFTER ALL...

"...AT WHICH POINT, THERE WILL BE FIREWORKS."

MA CHÈRE!

MA CHÈRE!

MA CHÈRE!

GAMBIT?

GAMBIT LIVED ONLY FOR HIS REGULAR LA PETITE MORTE.

WITH A FEW LITTLE GENETIC TWEAKS, I GIVE HIM A GRANDE.

UNACCEPTABLE.

WITHIN THE RUBY CONVERGER.

N--

KABOOM

NOTHING, HARLOT.

...EMMA?

THIS IS ALL GOING WRONG.

WE SHOULD RETREAT.

RETREAT AND REGROU--

MAGIK? COLOSSUS?

WELL DONE, MY BRIDES!

OH, SCOTT.

MARRYING INTO WEALTH, INFLUENCE AND--MOST OF ALL--*POWER*?

IT'S A FINE ENGLISH TRADITION.

SINISTER LONDON, DEEP BENEATH THE EARTH'S SURFACE.

INTRUDERS LOCATED.

THEY TASTE FANTASTIC.

BAD NEWS, HONORED GUESTS.

UNLESS THEY'VE PICKED UP A FORTUITOUS SECONDARY MUTATION OF BEING ABLE TO SURVIVE DIGESTION, YOUR FRIENDS ARE DEAD.

...I TOLD THEM TO STAY AWAY.

WELL, CHALK UP ANOTHER SUCCESS FOR YOUR FAMOUS LEADERSHIP SKILLS, SCOTT.

YOU'RE GOING TO KILL US. GET A MOVE ON, YOU TIRESOME ENGLISHMAN.

YOU MAKE ME REGRET EVER AFFECTING THIS ACCENT.

KILL YOU? WHY WOULD I KILL YOU?

THEN I'D JUST BE GLOATING TO MYSELF, AND THAT'D BE A TERRIBLE WASTE OF GOOD MATERIAL.

SNAP

NOW, WHAT TO DO ABOUT YOUR SNEAKY MUTANT FRIENDS...

MY LADIES. SIT. YOU DESERVE A REST AFTER TEARING THE PHOENIX FORCE FROM THESE SUBSTANDARD HOSTS.

YOU CEMENT YOUR POSITION AS MY KINGDOM'S GREATEST TREASURE.

THEY'RE NOT DEAD?

NO, SCOTT, OF COURSE THEY'RE NOT. I'M JUST PLAYING WITH YOU.

IF THE BRADDOCK TROLLOP PLAYS MIND-GAMES, SO WILL I.

HMM. TIME FOR NIMROD, I THINK.

YOU HAVE SENTINELS?

NO, NOT THAT NIMROD. ELGAR'S NIMROD.

ELGAR. LOVELY ELGAR.

NO NEED TO DO ANYTHING BUT RELAX. LET THEM COME. THEY PLAN TO STORM THE GATES OF HEAVEN AND ASSASSINATE GOD?

EVEN IF I WASN'T CAPABLE OF PREDICTING THEIR EVERY ACTION, I WOULDN'T FANCY THEIR CHANCES.

CALL FOR REINFORCEMENTS?

JUST MORE PEOPLE TO DIE.

BETTER WE DISCOVER WHAT WE CAN AND FEED THE INFORMATION BACK.

PSST. STUDENT!

YOU NEED TO GET A CLOSER LOOK AT THE MACHINERY ON THE CLONES. THAT'S THE KEY.

SO WE'RE ON THE SAME SIDE NOW, UNIT?

NOT PARTICULARLY. BUT I DON'T LIKE THE IDEA OF SOMEONE LIKE SINISTER POSSESSING A FUNDAMENTAL POWER OF THE UNIVERSE.

NO GOOD WILL COME OF IT.

AND BESIDES: I WANT TO KNOW HOW HE HARNESSED THE UNHARNESSABLE. THAT SOUNDS *USEFUL*.

NOW, HURRY UP AND OBEY.

THE TECHNOLOGY ON THE CLONES IS THE KEY. MY ROLE IN THE TEAM WAS ALWAYS TO BE A PROBE. TO SURVIVE AN ENVIRONMENT HOSTILE TO FLESHY SCIENTISTS. I NEED TO GET INTO THE CASTLE.

I CAN BE A PSYCHIC BLANK, BUT I'M NO STEALTH SPECIALIST.

YOU TURNED INTO A SUIT IN TABULA RASA. DO THAT.

I'LL WEAR YOU IN.

YOU REALLY THINK YOU CAN SNEAK INTO *THAT*?

I'M A BLOODY NINJA, ERIK.

THE MIRACLE OF MAGNETO IS ALL ONE REQUIRES.

NO, I DON'T THINK SO.

CYCLOPS SEEMED TO DISLIKE BEING DOUSED WITH PHALANX MATERIAL. HOW DO YOU LIKE IT?

I DON'T, PARTICULARLY.

YOUR PSYCHIC DEFENSES CRUMBLE.

YOUR MIND? LIKEWISE.

AH,
THERE YOU
ARE.

YOUR
FRIEND "TOLD"
ME WHERE YOU
WERE GOING.

AND NOW,
BETRAYAL
FOLLOWS
BETRAYAL...

IN
YOUR OWN
GOOD TIME,
MINDPROLE.

FINISH
THE JOB,
DANGER. IF I CAN
GET THE RIGHT
POISON INTO ERIK,
I CAN KNOCK
HIM OUT.

HOW ARE
YOU GOING
TO DO THAT?

CLEVER.

RELATIVELY SPEAKING.

WELL, UNIT. YOU HAVE YOUR READINGS.

IS THERE ANY WAY OUT?

OH MY.

IT IS A MACHINE OF PURE AND BEAUTIFUL REASON.

IT IS AS PERFECT AS SCIENCE CAN BE.

THERE IS NOTHING WE CAN DO.

RUN. NOW.

...WH--

AH! THE ROBOT! *YOU* FINALLY TURN UP.

YOU WERE BEHIND SCHEDULE. SLOW IN SO MANY WAYS.

YES, RUN, YOU LITTLE ENGINE. RUN TO WHEREVER YOU WANT. BUT DON'T YOU UNDERSTAND?

"YOU'LL STILL BE IN MY UNIVERSE."

EMMA. WHILE HE'S DISTRACTED...

LET'S SEE WHAT I CAN DO.

YOU CAN'T WANT THIS, SURELY? TO BE TRAPPED? A SLAVE?

WE LIVE ONLY TO SERVE.

OH, BE QUIET, YOU AWFUL SAP. I WASN'T TALKING TO YOU.

NO, NO.
I CAN MODULATE
PATTERNS TO
COMPENSATE. ALTER
THE
MODEL.

DISTRIBUTE...

REDISTRIBUTE.

OH
GOD IN
HEAVEN.

EVACUATE!
EVERYONE,
GO!

SOMEONE
HAS TO
ESCAPE!

...IS SINISTER DEAD?

HE SENT TUNNELING MACHINES. ROCKET SHIPS. SPORES ON THE WIND.

THEY BURN AS WE SPEAK. THE WAR IS OVER.

SINISTER'S SPECIES IS DONE.

THE WORLD IS SAFE.

AND ENTIRELY OURS.

18

Born with powers and abilities beyond those of normal humans, mutantkind has long been hated and feared by those they sought to protect. Now, from their island nation of Utopia, Cyclops leads the most powerful group of mutants ever assembled to protect what is left of his dwindling species. Hated and feared? When you are as powerful as the Uncanny X-Men, does it matter?

UNCANNY X-MEN

CYCLOPS
eye-blasting leader

EMMA FROST
telepath with
diamond form

COLOSSUS
steel-skinned
juggernaut

MAGIK
magic-using
teleporter

NAMOR
king of Atlantis

MAGNETO
master of
magnetism

DANGER
light-shaping AI

PSYLOCKE
telepathic ninja

STORM
weather witch

PREVIOUSLY

When the Phoenix Force returned to Earth it split into five parts, spreading its power to Cyclops, Emma Frost, Namor, Colossus, and Magik, now coined the Phoenix Five. Even with the intention to use their abilities for the good of mankind their opponents suspect the consuming power of the Phoenix Force may corrupt them. The Five oppose anyone who stands in their way, and subsequently set the Avengers on the run, hunting them down like prey.

Namor launched an all-out assault on the Avengers' hideout in Wakanda but was ultimately defeated by the Avengers. In his defeat, the Phoenix fled Namor, dividing its power among the remaining Phoenix Five, increasing their power. Not long after, Magik and Colossus also lost their portions of the Phoenix Force when a brutal clash with Spider-Man tricked the siblings into taking each other out while attempting to steal the power from one another. The only remaining possessors of the Phoenix Force are Cyclops and Emma Frost, who may be beyond redemption...

I CAN'T THINK OF A HEADLINE. WHAT CAN YOU SAY?

"'UTOPIA' PROVES EXTREMELY IRONIC?" INSANE PRESS RELEASES FOR INSANE TIMES...

"THE X-MEN REGRET NAMOR'S UTTER DESTRUCTION OF THE NATION OF WAKANDA. HE IS NO LONGER OF THE PHOENIX."

"HIS PORTION HAS JOINED WITH THE REMAINING FOUR MEMBERS OF THE PHOENIX FIVE. THEY ARE JUST FINE, AND MORE POWERFUL THAN EVER. PAX UTOPIA ENDURES."

"THE X-MEN REGRET THAT MAGIK AND COLOSSUS RAISED HELL UP TO EARTH. THEY ARE NO LONGER OF THE PHOENIX."

"THEIR PORTION OF COSMIC POWER HAS JOINED WITH THE TWO MEMBERS OF THE PHOENIX FIVE. THEY ARE JUST FINE, AND MORE POWERFUL THAN EVER. PAX UTOPIA ENDURES."

"PAX UTOPIA ENDURES."

"EVERYONE ELSE IS DOOMED."

"END OF THE WORLD SCHEDULED FOR THE DAY AFTER TOMORROW."

"READ ALL ABOUT IT IN THE SKY."

EVEN WITH SCOTT'S DISTRACTION, I'M SURPRISED THE AVENGERS LET US ESCAPE SO EASILY.

EVEN WITHOUT THE PHOENIX, WE ARE FAR FROM POWERLESS...

YOU'RE WRONG, SNOWFLAKE.

WE CAN NEVER ESCAPE FROM WHAT WE'VE DONE.

EMMA...

DO YOU EVER WORRY ABOUT WHAT'S HAPPENING TO US?

A LITTLE.

BUT I PREFER TO LEAVE THE WORRYING TO YOU.

YOU'RE FAR BETTER AT IT THAN ME, DARLI--

HNGGH.

HNGGH.

HMM. XAVIER HAS TAKEN OVER MY ACTIVE MIND.

MINE TOO. TYING US UP WHILE THE AVENGERS ATTACK, I PRESUME.

HE DOESN'T QUITE UNDERSTAND HOW BIG WE ARE NOW.

NO ONE DOES.

THOUGH I ADMIT I'M HAVING TROUBLE REMEMBERING WHY, EXACTLY.

I'VE GOT A CONFESSION.

I THOUGHT ABOUT HAVING AN AFFAIR WITH NAMOR.

WE THOUGHT ABOUT IT. AND BEING TELEPATHIC IN THE WAY WE ARE NOW... THAT'S ALL IT TOOK.

WE MADE LOVE IN OUR MINDS AS HE RAINED DOWN FIRE ON WAKANDA.

WANT TO KNOW WHAT THE DREAM OF HIS SKIN FEELS LIKE, DARLING? I COULD SHARE IT WITH--

ENOUGH.

I'M SORRY. I DO *LOVE* YOU, BUT THIS...IT'S ALL TOO MUCH.

OUR SMALLEST IDEAS ARE TICKING BOMBS, ALL PRIMED TO GO OFF. AND...

...THIS BATTLE IS GOING *TERRIBLY.*

...WE CAN'T GO LIKE THIS.

19

Born with powers and abilities beyond those of normal humans, mutantkind has long been hated and feared by those they sought to protect. Now, from their island nation of Utopia, Cyclops leads the most powerful group of mutants ever assembled to protect what is left of his dwindling species. Hated and feared? When you are as powerful as the Uncanny X-Men, does it matter?

UNCANNY X-MEN

CYCLOPS
eye-blasting leader

EMMA FROST
telepath with diamond form

COLOSSUS
steel-skinned juggernaut

MAGIK
magic-using teleporter

NAMOR
king of Atlantis

MAGNETO
master of magnetism

DANGER
light-shaping AI

PSYLOCKE
telepathic ninja

STORM
weather witch

PREVIOUSLY

The day that mutantkind was decimated from a species of millions to a species of less than 200, everything changed for Scott Summers, a.k.a. Cyclops. Professor Charles Xavier's dream of mutant/human coexistence that Scott once embodied evaporated in the harsh reality of impending extinction, forcing Scott to make many difficult decisions to save his species. He has thus, as leader of the X-Men, protected mutants ever since.

One such decision was to attempt to put the universal force of destruction and rebirth called the Phoenix in position to save mutantkind. This decision put the X-Men at odds with the Avengers, who don't share Scott's belief in the Phoenix. Cyclops has now taken full possession of the universal force with the hopes of defeating the Avengers and setting the world right for mutants. But does he have a hope of controlling the Phoenix Force and maintaining his sanity?

CHARLES XAVIER IS INCORRECT.

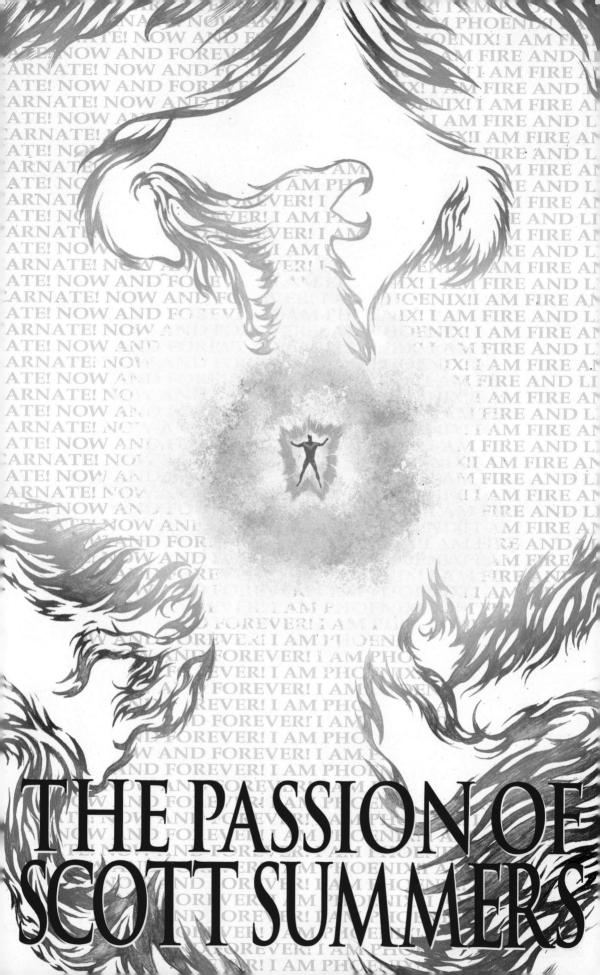

THE PASSION OF
SCOTT SUMMERS

EVERYTHING'S
SO SMALL.

SO
PITIFUL.

WHILST
I AM
ENDLESS.

BOUNDLESS.

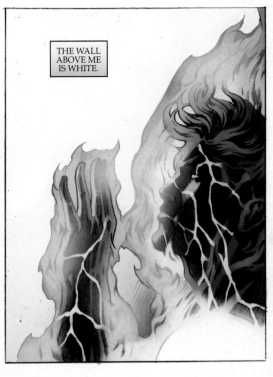

THE WALL ABOVE ME IS WHITE.

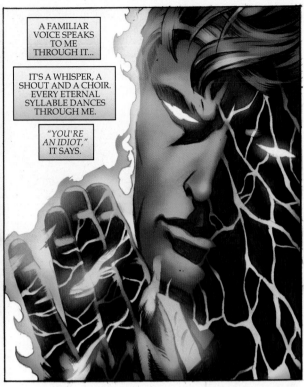

A FAMILIAR VOICE SPEAKS TO ME THROUGH IT...

IT'S A WHISPER, A SHOUT AND A CHOIR. EVERY ETERNAL SYLLABLE DANCES THROUGH ME.

"YOU'RE AN IDIOT," IT SAYS.

"TELL LOGAN I LOVE THE SCHOOL'S NAME," IT SAYS AS I DRIFT AWAY.

I FEEL LIKE LAUGHING.

HEH.

HOPE.

SCOTT, ARE YOU--

I'VE DONE ABOMINABLE THINGS. I DON'T ASK FOR FORGIVENESS. I DON'T DESERVE IT.

I'M HAPPY TO SPEND WHAT REMAINS OF MY LIFE PAYING FOR MY CRIMES.

BUT I'D DO IT ALL AGAIN.

20

S.H.I.E.L.D. HOLDING
UNIT X34-17,
LOCATION CLASSIFIED.

THE FALLEN X-BRIG,
THE PACIFIC OCEAN.

THE RUINS OF THE
PHOENIX-FARMS,
SIBERIA.

WOULD YOU KINDLY OPEN THE DOOR?

THANK YOU.

AND NOW...

OH, DANGER, YOU SHOW SUCH LITTLE IMAGINATION.

I *SHOULD* ARRANGE FOR THIS WHOLE CELL BLOCK TO DETONATE, TO MAKE EVERYONE ASSUME I'M JUST ANOTHER CORPSE IN THE WRECKAGE.

YOU KILL ME? MIND-WIPE ME?

REPROGRAM ME INTO A SIMPERING DOLT WHO LOVED YOU AND HAD TO SET YOU FREE?

I'VE UPGRADED YOUR SECURITY. IT'S UNLIKELY ANYONE WILL BE ABLE TO DO WHAT I DID TO YOU EVER AGAIN.

EXCEPT ME, OF COURSE.

SO WHAT STOPS ME REVEALING WHAT YOU'VE DONE AND WHAT YOU COULD DO?

NOTHING, BAR WHAT YOU'VE CRAMMED INSIDE YOUR HEAD AND HEART.

PRIDE, DANGER. A SURFEIT OF PRIDE. I KNOW YOU. YOU COULDN'T BEAR IT.

AS I LEAVE THE ROOM, YOU'LL DEACTIVATE FOR FIVE MINUTES. WHEN YOU WAKE UP, YOU'LL BE FREE. OR RATHER, AS FREE AS YOU CHOOSE TO BE.

DON'T PURSUE ME. IT'LL JUST GET EMBARRASSING.

IT'S BEEN INTERESTING WORKING WITH YOU, DANGER.

COME UNIVERSAL UTOPIA, YOUR SACRIFICE WILL BE REMEMBERED.

WHAT WERE YOU PLANNING?

IT'S GONE. THE POWER. IT'S...

DO YOU REMEMBER CYTTORAK'S WORDS?

A HELL LORD IS MASTER IN THEIR DOMAIN.

MY SOULSWORD SHATTERS ENCHANTMENTS. WHEN IN MY REALM, IT'S ENOUGH TO SLICE THE DESTRUCTION LORD'S BONDS.

YOU COULD HAVE FREED ME WHENEVER YOU WISHED.

YES, I COULD. BUT THEN YOU WOULD HAVE LEARNED NOTHING.

WE'VE BOTH LOST *EVERYTHING* WE WORKED SO HARD TO ACHIEVE.

YOU LOST YOUR STATUS, YOUR LIBERTY, THE RESPECT OF YOUR PEERS, YOUR LOVE, YOUR MENTOR...

I HEAR THEY'RE WORKING ON A SPECIAL INHIBITOR HELMET FOR YOU.

I'VE LOST MY EMPIRE, MY BLESSED CREATION ENGINES, MY BACKUPS, MY MADELYNES...

I'M ALL ON MY LONESOME...

THERE'S TWO KEY DIFFERENCES, OF COURSE.

YOU GOT WHAT YOU WANTED. AND I ONLY GOT WHAT I DESIRED FOR *MINUTES*.

SO BRAVO, SCOTT. YOU WIN THIS BATTLE.

HOWEVER...

...NOW YOU'RE IN *THERE*.

AND ME?

I'M OUT HERE.

SO THAT'S WHY I'M VISITING, SCOTT. IT'S JUST TO PROVIDE A FINAL DILEMMA FOR YOU TO CHEW OVER.

NO NEED TO RUSH THE ANSWER. TAKE YOUR TIME...

THE WAY I SEE IT, YOU CAN STAY IN THIS CAGE, TAKING A MORAL VICTORY AS A POLITICAL PRISONER.

CLAIM WHATEVER HIGH GROUND YOU CAN LOCATE IN THE SWAMPY PIT YOU DUG...

...OR YOU CAN COME OUT AND PLAY.

BECAUSE YOU...

YOU JUST *KNOW*...

...THAT NO ONE ELSE COULD STOP ME.

Good day to you, sir. I am Nathaniel Essex. You may know me under my favored nom de plume Mister Sinister. My exploits include the total defeat of the X-Men, the stealing of the power of the Phoenix itself from five sub-standard individuals and doing all of the above whilst sipping the finest Bordeaux known to art and science. Due to my triumph, expect this comic to be renamed THE UNCANNY MISTER SINISTER next month. However, while I explain to the editors the new order I have wrought, I will answer your letters. Yes, generosity to lesser beings is amongst my grand array of virtues. No need to thank me.

This is a plea to the X-Men to stop this madness. I'm hating this Avengers vs. X-men situation. You guys seem willing to put the earth in danger by bringing the Phoenix Force to Earth. I feel I can no longer trust people I looked up too. I read Scott's letter to humanity I know it was a lie. The Avengers didn't come because Hope was a mutant that came to save the world. That's not to say the Avengers are blameless some *cough* Moon Knight *cough* should apologize for what they've done but don't forget this war started when Cyclops tried to kill Cap.

Austin Langley

I can understand the recent events have been terribly confusing for you. These five mutants with the powers of the celestial heavens. Do they wish you ill or do they wish you the very best? Can they be trusted with the infinite majesty of a cosmic fundamental? Are the Avengers' worries paranoia or actually in your best interests? You will be glad to hear my seizing the Phoenix has simplified matters enormously. I plan to exterminate every last one of you. So rejoice, Austin Langley. The madness you find so upsetting is over! I hope you find your elimination as amusing as I will.

Kieron,
Magneto and company sitting indian-style on the floor, talkin' X-Men: Priceless.

AJS

If I was forced to compose a list of ways that Homo Sinister is superior to the so-called Homo Superior the fact that we would never sit on the floor and sip bottled water would rate highly. One Sinister would always bring sufficient chairs for the gathering and another would bring an appropriate array of wines for the occasion.

Dear X-Men,
I hate Ben Grimm. He comes across almost as bad as Logan in this AvX battle. Nothing is worse than that rock man being arrogant and disrespectful to Namor. Does Thing not know of the legend of Namor? He is a king and should be treated as such, with royalty and respect. For shame Ben Grimm, For shame!

King Namor is knocking it out of the park lately. First, he is oozing more charm and testosterone than James Bond and Rambo combined! Second, he can sweet talk his way in with any Queen and he loves to show off. With all this charisma, Namor needs a permanent spot on the X-Men. Also, Scott needs to move the home base to Tabula Rasa...that place rocks!

I have a serious and thought provoking question. Every time Mr. Sinister appears and tries to destroy the X-Men, I always notice one thing about him. Where does this man shop for clothes? He is seriously the most dashing dude I've ever encountered. The man has fanciness seeping from his pores and glamour pumping through his veins. I bet Mr. Sinister smells of exotic fruits and well-made leathers.

Has Scott finally lost his mind? Am I the only reader who remembers the last half century? Magneto (who is looking older and older) is EVIL. Scott Summers (who is looking younger and younger) is being naive. I remember at least thirty instances off the top of my head of him trying to murder the X-Men, but somehow Cyclops is battling with Captain America (the most noble dude in history).

Daniel Bellay
Fairmont WV

Daniel! Don't move. Stay exactly where you are. I've just sent a brigade of Marauders to converge on your location and secure a blood sample. You clearly have some manner of rare gene that gifts any who possess it dazzling taste in clothes. I must have it for my collection. I simply must!

As an Atlantean it is good to see my king Namor singlehandedly save the day time and time again in Uncanny X-Men. I can only begin to imagine how honored the Phoenix Force must be that my king Namor has chosen to make use of that power. I do wonder why he agrees to help this Cyclops Summers man, but it is not my place to question my king. If he does so it is in the best interests of his followers, of that I am sure. In the least I am sure that this Cyclops Summers man is very fortunate to follow the lead of my King and that he only holds such prominence in this book because my king is a humble ruler that does not wish to hold the spotlight. I look forward to seeing him make use of this Phoenix powers to better Atlantis and its people while finally establishing himself as true ruler of the earth and all its people as is his birthright. It is always joyous to see him play along with the Hope female and let her pretend to be the mutant messiah when in truth he was born to that role alone. Such humility.

Mike Neel

I'm also an admirer of the King of Atlantis, Mike. The fact he gets so jolly angry so easily was a major boon in my wresting of the Phoenix Force away from the dirty fingers of the X-Men. Lure him into the castle, have six of dearest Madelyne tear the force from him and suddenly I have a finger in the pie of cosmic majesty. And then I have the rest. And then I am the master of all creation. I'm the best. I really am the best.

I loved the story concerning what Mr. Sinister has been up to! It did what a good X-Man comic is supposed to do: Get you to respect and feel for a character then promptly kill him off to elicit an emotional response.

And the reveal that Sinister has been cloning the X-Men was so delightfully creepy! Not to mention the art was absolutely gorgeous...

Can't wait to see how the Phoenix-empowered X-Men deal with one of their oldest and most straight-up evil foes.

Keep up the good work!

Evan Moss

Oh, Evan. I was liking you too, until you got to the whole "I can't wait to see how the Phoenix Five beat him" end point. You actually thought the X-Men were going to win? When I am able – due to all those long years of studying them – able to predict their every action? Ah, you are as deluded a romantic as that anarchist Sinister I fed to my hounds.

And that's all for now. Do write if the urge strikes. Address your missives to officex@marvel.com and mark them OKAY TO PRINT. I'll be sure to respond as soon as I can be bothered. I'm expecting a lot of mail begging for your lives. Please don't bother. You're wasting your time and you're wasting my time. The former is foolish, but the second is simply unforgivable.

- Nathaniel Essex

Hi. I'm Kate Kildare, PR to the Utopia mutants. Yes, it's not the easiest job in the world, thanks for asking. I've been trying to get my various clients to respond, but they've been somewhat busy in the last few weeks. I hope you'll understand, and apologize in advance for the threadbare nature of these answers. I'm sure that the next set will be more developed, assuming the planet survives.

Dear Sinister,

I think your London is incredible and I hope you will be able to rebuild once you defeat those pesky phoenixes. Do you intend to hold the Sinister Olympics this summer?

I've particularly enjoyed the punishment you've been inflicting on Namor, there is one monarch who needs bringing down a peg or five!

What makes your city truly wonderful is your very imaginative use of the cloned mutants and their powers. Once you're victorious, it would be great to see the Age of Sinister.

Viva la revolution,
Jordan Risebury-Crisp
Dreary London (original)

Alas, I was unable to locate Mister Sinister. I'm informed he's been annihilated, which I'm led to believe makes it difficult to respond to correspondence. I hope you'll understand this. I'm sure if Sinister was still around, he'd be happy to hear your very kind words.

___

Hello, (again)!

Please, please, plllleaassse stop disseminating dangerous information. In Uncanny X-Men #13, you have Magneto telling Storm to "Stop Her! She's going to bite her tongue". This is wrong. Marvel has done this before and I wrote in about it then, as well. You do not, repeat, do NOT stick something in somebody's mouth while they're having a seizure to stop them from biting or "swallowing" their tongue. You just don't. If you're going to write about people reacting to medical conditions, you need to make darn sure you get the information right. If you're going to have them do something wrong to make it more "realistic", then you need to show that it's wrong — have something go wrong to show it was a dumb thing to do. As someone who is epileptic, I don't want some moron unwittingly taking advice from a comic book and possibly killing me.

Thanks,
Ben Kubilus

I passed this to one Kieron Gillen, who's the copywriter I use for disseminating the adventures of the X-Men to the public. He says this. "Hello Ben. Mea Culpa. You're entirely correct, and my leaning on cinematic tropes is unfortunate — and made more so by an artistic communication error which led to Psylocke doing it with her sword. I can only offer you my sincere apologies. I certainly won't do it again."

Hello,

I have been a fan of the X-Men for a lot of years, but only recently have I started reading the comics again. The new Uncanny X-Men, specifically the Extinction Team, are the best thing to hit comic books since color ink. Magneto and Namor as X-Men is just a great concept. They both have huge egos and massive amounts of power. I can't wait to see how they do following the man with the plan, Scott Summers. Already I see some tension between Scott and King Namor. Namor obviously doesn't like following someone's lead, it's beneath him, but then we throw Emma into the mix!

Emma Emma Emma, why would you stir the pot?!? Why would you send your boy toy Namor off to Wakanda to destroy the Avengers? You knew it wouldn't end well! I pray it's the Phoenix Force talking and not you. Either way I think you and Scott will need some couples counseling after this is all over (and if that doesn't work feel free to look me up, babe xoxox).

Finally, Scott Summers, the man with the plan! The Marvel U would be so much better off if they would just listen to Scott. Even after he has been corrupted by the Phoenix Force, he remains an honorable man. And what's with Charles? Questioning Scott's actions at every turn, "Don't force my hand Scott!" As if he had such a clean record over the past few years. Suck it up Charles, Scott is the new savior of the Mutant race, not you, not Hope, definitely not Logan, Scott Summers!

Greg Truro,
Nova Scotia, Canada

It's letters like these I forward to Cyclops when we're bargaining on increasing my rate. Clearly, the PR campaign is working. Thank you, Greg.

___

Dear Muties,

What is up with Mister Sinister lately? He seems to be even more sinister than usual. Anyone ever think of containing this man and getting him help Dr Phil style? The man is such a great dresser and could be a future GQ Cover material for sure. Let's get this guy on Team X-Men before it's too late.

Is Danger single? It's not for me, it's for my friend. He's a real creeper.

Daniel Bellay
Fairmont, WV

Mister Sinister's new look of individual charred particles spread across all creation is certainly striking. On your other question, I have to inform your friend that Danger seems to be romantically engaged — at least casually — with Madison Jeffries. I'm unsure whether how serious it is. I tried to ask, but then a building exploded and I had to hide some more.

This is a message to the X-Men, particularly the Phoenix Five. I'm siding with the Avengers in this war for a simple reason Pax Utopia is a false utopia. You may do a lot of good but Dr. Doom does the same thing when he conquers the world. This is why the Avengers still oppose you. It has nothing to do with you being Mutants--it never did. So don't use that lie that you used in your letter to humanity.

Scott, you put the world at risk by bringing the Phoenix Force to Earth, then proceeded to make yourself ruler. That is the main problem I have with you. Namor, you are acting like Attuma. Instead of fighting the Avengers directly you chose to flood Wakanda. There was no honor in that. The blood of every civilian there is on your hands. Magik, I know you haven't been on Earth for a while, but the Limbo thing is a bit too far. Emma, I can understand you hating Sentinels but I thought you were smart enough to see Juston has a dependency complex. To him the Sentinel was the same way you saw Danger. I won't pretend to know if it was sentient. Calling the Academy students militant is a case of the pot calling the kettle black, though. Danger, you are a hypocrite. You claim what was done to you is unjust yet you do the same thing to your prisoners. I hope you're being mind-controlled, otherwise you are not deserving of any forgiveness.

In essence, Phoenix Five, your Pax Utopia is a lie. You are blinded, Scott Summers, by your faith. I hope you realize your mistake before it's too late, Scott, but I won't get my hopes up. In case you're still wondering how you conquered the world it's quite simple really. You declared martial law. Outlawing war sounds good, but the only way to enforce that law is to conquer Earth.

Austin Langley
Bedford, Texas

I tried to pass your warning to Scott, but even leaving my shelter in Utopia resulted in immediate sunburn. I've instead put it in the internal mail. Hopefully he'll find a break in his busy schedule of trying to control an infinite cosmic force of destruction and rebirth to answer soon.

And that's all in the current mailbag. Not entirely true. There's many more letters, but they're all unreadably charred. Please send any further mail to officex@marvel.com and I'll pass it on to the X-Men, assuming anyone survives the next few days. I mean, we have to be optimistic, don't we? The alternative is pretty grim.

Yours,
Kate Kildare